THREADS:

Poetry to Inspire Art

THREADS:

Poetry to Inspire Art

Poets of Queens Press and Yara Arts Group
New York, 2023

Designed and composed by Oleksandr Fraze-Frazenko.
Art by: Aze Ong
Photograph by: Pavlo Terekhov
Cover design: Waldemart Klyuzko

ISBN 978-1-7351478-8-8

CONTENTS

Pichchenda Bao is a Cambodian American poet and writer. Her work has been published by *the New Ohio Review*, *the Ilanot Review*, *Cultural Daily*, *the Coop: A Poetry Cooperative*, *the West Trestle Review*, *the Adirondack Review*, *great weather for MEDIA*, *Newtown Literary*, *the Cambodian American Literary Arts Association* and elsewhere. She has received fellowships and support from Aspen Words, Kundiman, Bethany Arts Community, and Queens Council on the Arts. She lives, writes and raises her three children in New York City. More at www.pichchendabao.com.

Mother Tongue

My mother said,
        When you were born,
        they kept saying you were black
        so I named you, Diamond.
Which is how I came to understand that black
wasn't precious enough to her.
My name was a shield, a cover, an irony.
She had borne the unbearable,
yet my dark skin was too much.
New mother, new baby, broken world,
but this scorn stayed intact.

The thing is
she was speaking in Khmer,
and Khmer words are slippery,
like memories.
                Kapek kapok.
If this is a true story,
what else can I remember?

The kitchen counter
cluttered with reused jars.
The smell of frying garlic.
Her slamming an old meat cleaver
through bone and sinew.
Our meals were full of shards
I quickly learned to pick out.

Another time, she said,
        Your father loved me
        until you were born.
Her face so full of longing
I knew she didn't see me.
My face like my father's face,
same shape and shadow.

One day she will tell me
she had always wanted a daughter first.
But not before she says,

Women can't be as smart as men.
She will say,

     I know these flowers die so quickly,
     but I want them anyway.

Zuihitsu For My Inconsistent Dreaming

In the dream I know is not a dream, I wait.

You walk out on me, and I want you to. A one-way door,
reckless with sorrow and relief.

But sometimes I don't feel anything at all.

 I'm looking for something. A bathroom. A jacket left behind.
   Something I needed to take care of. Something I know isn't
                                lost, but still can't find.

Sleep when the baby sleeps just means learn to live in
delirium. The baby doesn't sleep. She dreams.

            My son says he can't sleep, has never slept.
His body appears in the middle of the   night.
A hot compress at my back.

                I can't remember if I had been
dreaming or awake.

We are in my dreams. We party. We dance. We wait in line
for the bathroom. Then we get on the road, cramming
ourselves into a car that no one knows how to drive.

The thing about sleep is that everything remains unresolved.
Every time, morning arrives, and I'm still there,
lost in a car full of strangers I thought I knew,
wanting to get back.

Rosebud Ben-Oni is the author of several collections of poetry, including *If This Is the Age We End Discovery* (2021), which won the Alice James Award and was a Finalist for the National Jewish Book Award. She has received fellowships and grants from the New York Foundation for the Arts, CantoMundo and Queens Council on the Arts. Her work appears in *POETRY, The American Poetry Review, Academy of American Poets' Tin House, Guernica, Electric Literature,* among others. Her poem "Poet Wrestling with Angels in the Dark" was commissioned by the National September 11 Memorial & Museum in NYC. *In May 2022,* Paramount commissioned her video essay "My Judaism is a Wild Unplace" for a national campaign for Jewish Heritage Month. In 2023, she received a Café Royal Cultural Foundation grant to write *The Atomic Sonnets*, a full-length poetry collection based on her chapbook *20 Atomic Sonnets* (*Black Warrior Review*, 2020). In January 2023, she performed at Carnegie Hall on International Holocaust Memorial Day, as part "We Are Here: Songs From The Holocaust."

All That Is and Is Not Nuclear Is Our Family

I highly recommend disconnecting.
I realize the strangeness of telling you over a connection.
But here comes and goes, so I have to send things when it's working.
Things are a little rough.
In cities I am everywhere.
I don't get lonely. I lose faith that how things are
Are also how things will always be. In forever uphill rising
Streets I have a calling. She calls me from her high-rise
Office at the World Bank to warn me after ten years of *this,*
She's leaving Hong Kong—leaving *the country*—
For the week her in-laws visit.
You tell me that woman is not blood
Which means she should have nothing to say
About your family. This is not to say you
Do not treat me well. You humor me
At the chichi dim sum place
Hidden away like a speakeasy. You eat everything
I order. Often I get a pass others do not. If I have too much
To drink, you say my best thing
Is one face, not two. This is not about saving face.
We get it all out in the open, you & I.
We aren't the kind to get lonely
When we fight. You say I can't help but look like things meant
To keep you in line. You say I always take your wife's side.
We are not bad people. We understand the difference.
Difference is flickering neon until the other loses sight.
Now I'm writing this on the rooftop in a little room
You built without permission, next to a washroom
You built to make me more comfortable. Early this morning
You squeezed through the crowds at the bakeshop
To bring me a red bean bun, right out of the oven.
You remind me fish is only fresh when alive
& gasping. On the rooftop, wild cockatoos
Eat the chichi seed I recommended to you.
You never make it in time to see them.
I want to be a good daughter to you.
But then my mind wanders & Icelandic horses
Disperse through Hong Kong skyline where blood-or-not nieces
& nephews clear out of their six-days-a-week offices.

Poetry, you say, is the furthest, furthest thing from you.
What long lines, where & why they break
You won't see. Here I have no grievances. I still see the island
In this city, & you correct me: *autonomous territory*.
Autonomy, we agree, is never real in full nor fully
Realized. I say it's like coming to know a new
Father. You say one day you want to be yourself
Around me. I say once in cities I was everywhere but here
I write to you in a little room while you make your deliveries.
Dinner tonight at your favorite Vietnamese place
& then shopping in a night market. Only your son
Would chose such neutral territory.
I study the map to Ladies Market, chart the longest route.
Because you ask me to lead. Because you say nothing
When I take the wrong street. I never ask for help.
You never say we are lost.

If This Is the Age We End Discovery
(Alice James Books, 2021) by Rosebud Ben-Oni

The Songs We Know Not to Talk Over

After a funeral, something wrestles from the wind,
Flutters haphazardly close to your aching chest.
Most likely it will fall to the cracked sidewalk.
Stop walking. Consider it. You won't understand
What you are looking at, this sort of green would-be
Katydid with dragonfly wings & limbs like a praying
Mantis. It's incapable of anything
But beginning. It won't sense your grief
For someone it has been. Walk away first.
You won't see it again. Because now it's a bird.
Not very scientific, but I have seen this. Not the
transformation,
But how often have I asked the sky
What comes after death & then two birds
Pass over my head. I couldn't tell you why
I awaken at times to a pecking
At my eyes. I don't know why some birds return
To haunt us. I have felt thin, small talons
Dig into my wrist. We tangle in the darkness,
Porous as loess. No trail of marigolds & copal incense.
No falconers in the boot hills. Where we go, I feel still
But never remember. In the morning a sparrow steals
A half-eaten donut from a pack of feral cats,
& I promise to spare the life of all that is winged.
I watch where I step & still a wasp stings.
I'm sorry. The only promises I've kept are those
Scientifically proven. I have no ion-infrared
Evidence, no delicate microphones to catch
When I check the closets & drains
During a thunderstorm, when I've said,
Sitting at a deathbed, it's gonna be okay.
I've told them not to pull the plug
Even if my body says when
Bury me standing, bury me
Three times. No one really drops dead from seeing
Your gaunt, flitting shape in the mirror.
Not mirror but grace. Forgive me for covering
My eyes, for cowering under the blanket, for swatting

At you when I passed a flower garden,
When I shut my windows & chased you
From park benches & fruit trees. I didn't know
There are people I'm not willing to ever let go,
& I won't. I haven't.

If This Is the Age We End Discovery
(Alice James Books, 2021) by Rosebud Ben-Oni

All Palaces Are Temporary Palaces

My niece calls with questions of asteroid mining.
At six she's worried & can't tell me why.
So we talk it out. I hear there is gold, silver, platinum
On spent comets. Who would say *I do* on a stony
Asteroid? People are already getting married underwater,
The very rich driving cars on coral reefs.
& if the newest frontiers require technology
Smaller than an atom, well, now there's the pentaquark
Which is almost all quark save for one
Antiquark, & if not for the anti-
Quark, would anything, any-
Thing at all, be? What's next is never
Enough. All left to chance shrinking. My dear, dear girl
Calling on this overcast day in the spring, where sky is one long cover
Of impassivity. *Why are we here?* She's asking for the first time,
& I hear the anxiety of one who's stumbled upon a burning
Temple in the fields. We listen to each other
Breathe. I miss my train, linger on a winding staircase
In Woodside, Queens. I remember the day I discovered
This small stretch of exposed track subverting the sky and knew
I'd come home. One more day, & I will tell her this.
One more day for life on asteroids without fences or fracking,
& dreams know no deep inelastic scattering. Let it be
Where silence is never summoned, where rays
Collide in charm & strange.

If This Is the Age We End Discovery
(Alice James Books, 2021) by Rosebud Ben-Oni

Sherese Francis (she/they) describes themselves as an Alkymist of the I-Magination, finding expression through poetry, interdisciplinary arts, workshop facilitation, editing, and literary curation. Her(e) work takes inspiration from her(e) Afro-Caribbean heritage (Barbados and Dominica), and studies in Afrofuturism and Black Speculative Arts, mythology and etymology. Some of their work has been published in *Furious Flower*, *Obsidian*, *Rootwork Journal*, *The Caribbean Writer*, *The Operating System*, *Cosmonauts Avenue*, *No Dear*, *Apex Magazine*, *Bone Bouquet*, African Voices, *Newtown Literary*, and *Free Verse*. Additionally, Sherese has published four chapbooks, *Lucy's Bone Scrolls* (Three Legged Elephant, 2017), *Variations on Sett/ling Seed/ling* (Harlequin Creature, 2018), *Recycling a Why That Rules Over My Sacred Sight* (DoubleCross Press, 2021) and Lady Liberty Smashing Stones (THRASH Press, 2022). Sherese was a finalist for the Furious Flower poetry prize (2020) and CAAPP Book Prize (2021), and won The Caribbean Writer's Vincent Cooper Literary Prize (2021) for the poem, "SomNuh/Mbulist (Patois Possession)." Sherese also has received grant awards from Queens Council on the Arts, NYFA and NYSCA and residencies from WorksonWater and LMCC. Besides publications, Sherese has had her(e) work featured in various exhibitions and showcases from The Lit Exhibit, NY Live Arts, Queens Public Library, York College Arts Gallery, King Manor Museum, WorksOnWater, Flushing Town Hall, Jamaica Center for Arts & Learning, Jamaica Flux, Baxter St Camera Club, Bliss On Bliss, Maleza Proyectos, The Rubenstein Art Center and Ely Center for Contemporary Art. For more info: https://linktr.ee/sheresefrancis

Orishanal NGLS

After JP Howard
YìN ORuKọ

Praise   the heavy load that has put a claim on your soul
Praise   the word its in vent ion like lava out of a
mountainous mouth
Praise   the read to be able to bend in the whirl'd essence of
ink in the body
Praise   the holy all saints as one fractured and found
broken and bound
Praise   the (K)Not   the life made when a point strings all
positions
Praise   the click   the way the tongue connects an abyss
between the lips
Praise   the water spinning soul around to switch on the
lightbulb I   Praise the sun   a fusion of many kin a
combustible cord a broken open
Praise   the reflection that breathed into a muddy earth like
aN (Af) Huuu Re KiN

Recycling A Why That Rules Over My Sacred Sight,
DoubleCross Press 2021

Ra Hurt Became a Grace Robber

GoNe SuN dressed up in a far away joke
the black and red yoke and my mind capped
in a bright yoga bend and blend:
I made the devil up
I doubled up and threw my body down
on souling my sol and crossing over
traded my old self for a new model
as I traveled with haunts on my path
learned the art
of hyperbolic parable
the guitar sing
the goo goo ga ga of tar
I sacrificed my time in a cemetery
I mastered my self
by stringing my self up
as giver and taker of sound
there's no instant spell
the real story won't excite you quickly enough
so here's my black and red cape
for a retelling of story to hook belief
the fine I play along with
and I cast Ike Z. Mr. I Am
bursting with laughter
rising from the tomb
as my carpenter

Recycling A Why That Rules Over My Sacred Sight,
DoubleCross Press 2021

JU/NKonnu Costum (Oko)NKo Je (Printing a Rag(Wo)man Tempest on a Pierrot Plate)

A Poetic Play/Zuihitsu Inspired by Ged Merino's Piece for the Threads Exhibition and Junkanoo Lithograph Sketches by Isaac Mendes Belisario

"I stole the torturer's tongue.
it's the first side of me some see
the first line you hear
first line of defense when I say
"See this long tongue illicitly acquired—
doesn't it suit me well?" — David C. Findlay's Stolen Tongue

Koo-Koo also known as Actor Buoy plays every part, dressed in de/finery
Pantomimes Shakespeare's white mas
Finds enjoyment in the grotesque habits of pain(t) and horns while dancing to Calypso
De/Scriptions of Performance: During a Krik Krak Mas around the Jack in the Green, a CouCou NT tree dressed in a bow and flags
On a ship at sea: a tempestuous noise of thunder and lightning heard
Where's the master?
To begin to solve the mystery, it is necessary to look south, past the border
When did the borders become fixed?

Peetie Rag(Wo)man:
Here are my reversions of a cheat!
Nobody to pass property to when a property is not claimed!
I can come and take! Finders Keepers of new-re/mem/bered riddims!
Dis is how to give a DiCtionary a MeLody! To charm a charmer!
How did Ju/NKonnu end up in North Carolina=Virginia=Bahamas=Jamaica=Axim(a)?

Ma'am Red Set-Lady:
To every art I call.
I bear de kinship; now on de beak,
now here in de waist — de waist holds a decktionary of Jab
Jabs.
I flamed. I a MaZe. I a divine ode.
Burnin in many places; on top de mas:
on logs, on legs, on logic, on locations!
De yawds and de extended whip,
that I flame, dis here and dat there!
Den I matta and ju/nk. Hear my voice like lightnin' kraks,
like dreadful thunder-claps, like waves tremble, see my
whip shake like a nebulous trident!

House John also known as Jaw-Bone:
I infect reason?

Ma'am Red Set-Lady:
Not a soul
But felt a fever of de mad and play'd
some tricks of desperation. Plunged in de foaming;
Den all me on fire: hair rising like reeds
and all de Jab Jab's are here!
Jemima, de blues-eyed jamette wit child;
Jemima captured de Jaw-Bone and made de Jaw-Bone tuk
wit de help of a minstrel band and a ragman child!
A dark figure in a human shape.
How does Jaw-Bone make de dark tuk?
Turn de anguish into language? Groan/odes
unlocking an eturnatty.

House John also known as Jaw-Bone:
Dare I tell you to be named Calypso of the sea?
Dare I tell you to be only seen by me?
Dare I tell you to turn us into a (K)Nub?

Ma'am Red Set-Lady:
To come across de yellow sands
and let de hands of wild waves
marry dem!
And be a slave to de familiar,
bonded to de house on de head!
For de strangeness in a story puts weight
On Dis_body!
And all the more it seeks to hide itself,
The bigger bulk it shows. Hence, bashful cunning!
Hear de cock crow:
CouCou Dorado Dub!

Ju/NKonnu:
Where de music come? In de body, de air, de water?
My kinship: a wreck. I gone mad! I vex!

Ma'am Red Set-Lady:
Bones at de bottom of de sea!
Hear dem now!

Peetie Rag(Wo)man:
How I carry de burden of wood? My voice loud like
thunder!
(Wit-in) Dere's wood enough wit-in.
How I infect de reason of Jaw-Bone? How I need to krik
krak
to feel my way through de dark. A snag has caught me
into madness and I see myself.
What am I here? *A man or a fish? dead or alive?*
a very ancient and fish-
like smell: I a reversion of a Ju/NKonnu. *A strange fish!*
A monster made man; an I lander suffering from de krik
krak
and a voice like thunder. I con jab of I land by de Jaw-Bone.
I am all de subjects dat he have!
You are a jesting monkey as much as I am.
Jaw-Bone — his helmet; a house full of books!
Here's witdom: never worship a fool full of intexicants as a
god,
but wit one long whip, I can batter his skull!

I rooted in an I will full of noises!
Listen to de band
And Dis voice loud like thunder!

House John also known as Jaw-Bone:
I taught a slave to lie; to respond to a whip and not my
kinship.
I play mas in MeLody with a pasteboard house of many
colors on my head.
I contort these limbs into a lawful equation, a self-evident
dressing of the body.

Peetie Rag(Wo)man:
You taught me l/anguish: to be conquered and crossed. I am
always running and crossing over. I should be a
Calypsonian Monarch on de Road March like Calypso Rose!

House John also known as Jaw-Bone:
I call all the egungun forth! Hear all the bones krik kraking
in the sea and roaring like thunder! My tricky spirit whose
feet leaves no prints has struck and traces a circle on the
ground for our feet dance wit-in!
*How do people commemorate events and lives that resist
entering into focus due to little or no written evidence of their
existence?*
*A body possessed of its social memory – call it a "spirit" – is a
body in some sense possessed of itself.*
*It is even possessed of itself as property, to put it in the
mystified but ennobling legal jargon whereby Anglo-
Americans claimed certain inalienable rights.*
*When there is no written record, the body becomes the
record.*
What is not erased is the body of memory.
*Are we only a mystery if one confines the search to the
borders of the state.*

Peetie Rag(Wo)man:
Oh de power of Jaw-Bone!

Ju/NKonnu:
I going to marry de Jab Jab's Daughta, a ragged MeLody, and
be his Sé/Mwen-In-Law to clear a path wit my whip and
cool myself when de mas is lifted.

House John also known as Jaw-Bone:
I have unknotted my whip and buried it in de ground! Its
sound plummets to de bottom where de bones krik krak!
My book drowns at de bottom of de ocean! Wit my krik
krak unknot, I am set free.

De Band Plays Mas: Minstrels of Fate: De elements
De Drums (Gumbay boxes)
De Fifes (Tiny flutes)
De Rasp (A piece of wood scrapped across a horse's
jawbone)
*"...began to beat their drums, to dance, and to sing, in a most
outrageous manner. The noise lasted all night, and prevented
us from falling asleep..."*
"...what, Massa, are we not to dance and make merry..."
*"...expressed my surprise, that having heard the word of God
for so many years, they still continued their heathenish
customs.."*

Krik Krak also known as M/udda Goddess:
De I is a many-colored messenger
It never disobey de web of Ju/Pierrot
Dis Mary/time Game in de ring
I knot and unknot
*The foundation [of his headdress] is an old hat, affording the
wearer the means of sustaining the superstructure, to which
it is firmly attached, and composed of various coloured beads,
bugles, spangles, pieces of looking-glass, tinsel, etc. attached
to a pasteboard form trimmed round the edges with silver
lace, surmounted with feathers. The garments are of muslin,
silk, satin, and ribbons.*

Peetie Rag(Wo)man:
Whatever de ground provides becomes an
igname=nyame=nambi ji=nommo
I see myself: an I in lickwid solution=a vital force of being

De small servant Sé/Mwen is de foundation of de kym
Shāh MāT: De kin(G) has been crossed and named
My costum is a chess board of many colors and Jemima is
my m/udda
Because dis CooCou Crow Dis Mary/time Game
I De iNQueror

Olena Jennings is the author of the poetry collection *The Age of Secrets* (Lost Horse Press, 2022) and the chapbook *Memory Project*. Her novel *Temporary Shelter* was released in 2021 from Cervena Barva Press. Her translation from Ukrainian with Oksana Lutsyshyna of *Nobody Knows Us Here, and We Don't Know Anyone* by Kateryna Kalytko was released in September 2022 from Lost Horse Press. Her translation of Vasyl Makhno's collection *Paper Bridge* was released in October 2022 from Plamen Press. Her translation with the author of Yuliya Musakovska's *The God of Freedom* is forthcoming from Arrowsmith Press. Her textile art has been shown at Bliss on Bliss Art Projects and the NYC Poetry Festival. She is the founder and curator of Poets of Queens.

INTO ETERNITY

She is everywhere.
He is sweeping pieces of her bone
that turned to dust

when the building
was bombed, her bed engulfed,
her solitude violated.

She had been between the sheets
in her underwear, writing in her journal
and tracing the shapes on her comforter,

her finger hovering over the fabric
as if she was doing embroidery,
a pattern her grandmother taught her.

When she was still a body, she often saw
him with a broom,
in front of a cafe,

brushing at cigarette butts
against a background of bright paint
that matched the sky.

It made her think of her day dreams.
He could sweep up their conversations,
the words they held in common.

The color yellow.
Zhovte

The bright sun eating away the bone.
Zhovte

A sunflower blossomed in endless fields.
Zhovte.

Her body became forever like this.

NEIGHBORS

We hear syllables
through the wall.
Mot –
her
a child cries
for
her/ in the vintage
suit.
Her/ whispering
words she types.
Her/ singing as she
sprinkles spice.
Her/ tending
the peonies.
She will scatter
petals
down the aisle
we are always
celebrating
our connection
as an insect
flies out their
window and into
ours.

CREATIVE LANGUAGE

I unearth something from the ground.
I am digging for beets,
but it is language.
The letters are covered in soil.
I put together words.
They are the words I spoke
to my grandparents, words
that crossed oceans and were
unchangeable.

Then there were new words.
Language blossomed in their mouths.
They sent me places that didn't
really exist because now the word did.
I played in imaginary realms
where I could really touch
the four walls. I wore imaginary clothes
and could really feel
the fabric.

It is now that I realize these words
are captured in my memory
though I have taught myself
not to use them.
My past has been unraveled
and I am living in the future
in the city where they were prone
to sickness. In the city where their
words are frozen like photographs.

Ananda Lima is a poet, fiction writer, and translator, the author of *Mother/land* (Black Lawrence Press), winner of the Hudson Prize, and four chapbooks: *Vigil, Tropicália,* winner of the Newfound Prose Prize, *Amblyopia,* and *Translation*. Her work has appeared in *The American Poetry Review, Poets.org, Kenyon Review Online, Gulf Coast, Pleiades, The Common, Witness*, and elsewhere. For her fiction, she was awarded the inaugural WIP Fellowship by Latinx-in-Publishing, sponsored by Macmillan Publishers, and an early version of CRAFT was named a finalist for the Restless Books Prize for New Immigrant Writing. She has an MA in Linguistics from UCLA and an MFA from Rutgers University, Newark. Originally from Brasilia, Brazil, she lives in Chicago. Her first collection of fiction, *CRAFT*, is forthcoming from Tor Books.

ARROYO
— *"Triste Bahia"* —

They say the first
letter of my name evolved
  from a picture of a
                      carcass
a cabeça de vaca
   sem as suas costelas
expostas like claws
   or jaws ancient
                      my
neighbor says not to
  let my son sleep
on my bed but I do
                      I
  know the terror
  at night we're haunted
  by my great great great
                      grand-
parents dry on cracked
soil beating in the cold
of my feet na Bahia in the
                      bones
  they inhabit on my bed
  In America, I learned
  that arroyos are
                   paths
  carved by the rain
  but I already knew
                   at
night the cracked soil
  calls for me, as
                   cabeças
de vaca of my greats
  calling and calling
                   I
  tell them *I don't
   know you,* but I
                   do

———————————

the city's spine
  is a split bifurcation
solidified in calcium
                  in
  America they
eat the bagasse of
  oranges and say my
                name
means bliss I am
  in love with bone white
concrete, the spine of the
                city
sits fleshless and free
  of scales flexible bones
that can bend and bend
             and
  keep bending and keep
bending and bending
  bending right up until they
             snap

After Nathaniel Mackey
and Caetano Veloso
(*Mother/land*, Black Lawrence Press)

Return

here
I am
back where it used to be
home the sky
-line of New York City
the east river underneath
like the next line in a poem
I am here
with my son again
with so many people
masked unmasked masks
dangling from their ears
baby blue paper white
returning soft
serve rainbow sprinkles
food trucks children tourists
us tourists he doesn't remember
it here, doesn't know that self
that baby I love that baby still him
like I am
still
me here and super
-posed elsewhere
like words
like *here* like *now*
written then
read
now here I am
eu sou so soul I am
in Queens I am still Lake
Michigan Vitoria
da Conquista Brasília
Itabuna Ilhéus The Dunes
Sewanee
and still
in my apartment
April 2020
fearful and hungry
for this

Queens
I press enter
return
to a new line
I am the baby
my mother knows
I am the mother
gone and unknowable
in the old yellowing photograph
I am
home
in Queens
I tell him *this place*
is also yours
here you put a rock in your mouth
here you stumble
your first steps over gravel
here you come out
of the house for the first time
newborn

Floraime Oliveros Pantaleta (b. 1994) explores the
contiguous boundaries of languages in lyrical,
linguistic, and exhibitionary modalities.

She published creative, critical, and research work in
local and international journals and has received a
fellowship from the Ateneo National Writers
Workshop in 2021. From 2020-2022, she served as
part of the National Committee on Literary Arts of the
National Commission for Culture and the Arts. Her
works have been part of the exhibitions *texture /
tendency* in Makati 2021, object orientations in Quezon
City 2023, and the *threads* iteration at
the Ukrainian Institute of Modern Art in Chicago
which will open from August 26 until October 22.

Currently, she is in Zamboanga City where she serves
as Executive Director of the Ateneo Zamboanga-
Mindanao Institute.

El año del perdida de juicio
The year of losing grip

Tapao de oscuro el una curva para na monte,
Na medio del oscuridad,
      tiene pampang onde puede hace cae cuerpo
      puede brinca, puede perde camino,
Tiene maga figura de gente ta kore na otro lao camino
tiene apretao amaro diila maga brazo
Ya mira tu el hora, tiene pa tu un poquito tiempo

Abla pa si mama, agacha para sabe dituyu posicion na terreno
el alreredor, ta aclara lang si talya daan na pensamiento
ya pruba tu bira cara, por que el pono pirmi ta culga de amaro
      que colgao tambien na gente desaparecido?
      Abla pa el maga Kristyano, ofrece lang daw kita maga reso
El pono connectao de amaro con pescuezo,
si Jim nombrao con negro pajaro

Muchu encuentro el ta socede na monte.
Tiene corrida del maga gente, almariada, busca ta comida
Muchu cortada de cabeza.

Cuanto vezes ya puede usa como veneno con el semilla?
      Entre medio del dos grande rama, ya tiene un calliada
      Greso el ojas na tierra, ya hace tumba con el pono, ya
corta con el mano
      ya esconde con el nicho.

Sabe tu ya cunta conmigo mi nana cae si ta tranca tu dituyu ojos,
ta puede tu conversa con el madre cacao. No hay le conmigo
abisa si cosa
      lang yo puede prigunta.
Antes tu espanta, anda llora, grita y gendeh ya bira
      hace buenamente el sueño. Nunca canaton llega edad de ciento
      Asegurao tu, canaton ba ta llama muerto?

*The Lock Raven Review, 49 Philippine-Language Poets in
Translation (Ed. Kristine Ong Muslim) with English
translation by Sigrid Marianne Gayangos*

Creolité

*"Comme l'Autre est la tentation du Même,
le Tout est l'exigence du Divers"*
- Édouard Glissant

To consent not to be a single being
is to declaim the effacement: aphasia.
Directly below your mimicry
is a plaster always molting. And
on a palimpsest is a secondhand memory
you prize for yourself.
So when the child comes up to you
with a gesture, owing from the rhythm
you do not recognize, you return a shrug.
Your language is *too* important.
In my utterance, I locate the erasure
and trace the faded pulses. We have replaced
it with makeshift words for the time being.
When you find a recollection, connect the synapses
for the whimper. A woman cried out
in a chortle, in search of the word for reticence,
tumbling for fraises of the fedantic.
With the waving of a hand—stop—or was it look?
was she asking us to look? Were we trembling?
When I return, it was just a matter of time
for a failure to recall. We oscillate between
and know only the middle. We are returning
to a space of vacuity. Of a wound and
we keep forgetting.

*Ubod 2020 by the National Committee on Literary Arts of the
National Commission for Culture and the Arts*

heteroglossia
refractions of Carlos Piocos III's Guerra Cantos

1. Y cosa tu ta puede pensa si ta conversa acerca del
    pellejo? Cada media noche, ta atraca kita na espejo y
    kita mismo gendeh ta conoce diaton cuerpo. Como
    nuevo vestido, ta estrania kita como estrangjero ta
    incuntra conoce con quien ya tarda ya no hay mira.
    Cuanto bilug el maga raya, el maga tajiada, maga marka
    de tringcada y onde estaba? Por que ba bien cerca el
    palabra piel na pelea? Ta principia acorda con cada unu
    mancha estaba na quema, ta nota todo ya sale
    mordedura del frio, ta caba consagra con todo maga
    irida estaba na maga nunca perde maga sintido. Como
    viuda estos maga marka na cuerpo. Y ahora con
    silencio, ay mira kita na unu y otro. *Gendeh yo ta busca
    guerra o encuentro,* ya sale na dituyu labio. *Puede ba yo
    entra na dituyu pellejo? Nomas tu man lingasa--yo ta
    busca lang era descanzo. Y tiene yo un ruego: habla tu
    ahora comigo, onde estaba este dituyu dinigrido? Donde
    parte con tigo siempre ta intumi? Por que se ta incha?
    Paquichura tu ya saca este irida?*

2. Tonight, a failure to recall is not forgetting. I knew you
    then with this body. Should you ask of loss, I could tell
    you how very little of you I can recollect. We saw eye to
    eye. And while I sat from across the room, you told me
    the mark by the corner of my eyelid meant I was
    scrupulous. I told you I met with strangers to do
    character study. You ask me why I had been shy. Did I
    do well as respite? Did I give you a story to think about
    while you're alone? While I rushed back with two more
    hours to spare at the terminal, I thought about how we
    were there shortly. Shortly, that was who we were.
    From where we slipped, I lost my footing. You made
    sure to time your kisses. You made sure I wanted some
    more.

3. Ipahintulot mong gisingin ko nang walang pag-
    aalinlangan ang iyong damdamin. Isusuko ko ang aking
    mga titig, sauladuhin ang bawat hakbang pabalik sa

iyo. Sa gabing iyon, lahat ay nasa tamang sukat: ang
dami ng mga salitang binitawan, ang puwang sa ating
mga hakbang, ang kawalang-imik sa gitna ng titigan,
ang daplis sa aking kamay bago magpaalam. Buntong-
hininga ang pagitan ng maningas na pandama.
Buntong-hininga ang puwang sa mga pagkukubli.
Buntong-hininga ang alaala sa ligalig ng gabi.

4.   Sa adlaw nga nahigugma ko ka nimo, nawala ang
     gabii—nikusog ang kainit, nihayag ang kalibutan. Ang
     paglungtad ninglapad, nidako aron mas daghan pa ang
     mohaum. Maihap na ang mga bitoon sa atong kwarto.
     Makatigom na kog mga gihay og dahon sa mga bulak,
     mga balod sa mga pangitaon na damgo, mga tingog sa
     gasiga nga saba. Mabati na nato ang walay kinutuban.
     Og sa kangitngit, anaay makakita na. Ang
     paghinumdumdum ko nimo walay kahangturan. Sama
     sa kawanangan, di na masukod pa.

5.   Puede ba yo toma el dituyu sueño? Manda ba tu comigo
     cura el dituyu irida usando di mio labio? Puede ba yo
     toma estaba na dituyu almario, dituyu soberbio? Puede
     ba yo tancha dituyu cara? Gendeh ba tu tiene miedo?
     Paquichura si este ya mismo diaton pellejo el diaton
     alma? Paquichura si amo ya ste el diaton ondo, diaton
     frivolo? Diaton saber y derecho? Paquichura si este ya
     el todo cosa tiene adentro? Paquilaya tu agara comigo?
     Paquimodo tu pruba tancha mi cuerpo?

6.   We pray to a dimly lit sky where the moon is not light
     but silhouette, a tear in the shroud created by a dagger.
     What are souls but apparitions of disembodied
     consciousness?

7.   Walang pahinga sa pagmamahal. Habang ang
     paghahalughog ay paghahanap ng pandamang mas
     sariwa, mananatili ang kalungkutan. Magmamasid pa
     rin ang kawalang-katiyakan. Magnanaknak ang
     nakakulob na dalamhati. Minsan, namamanhid lamang
     tayo sa sakit. O kaya'y magpapahintulot sa bawat
     nagpupuyos na pandama. Bumabalikwas sa sariling

paghinga. Ano nga ba ang pag-ibig kung hindi
pagbibihag? At ano nga ba ang mga hampas ngunit
isang mabangis na himas?

8. Sa imong damgo, nahitabo ang tanang niaging
    kalipay—naa pa ta sa kangitngit kung aha gasiga ang
    gabii. Pagsulod nako sa kalayo, nibuto ang dugay na
    nga gapuyo nga pagbati: Ikaw ang gabii na mas lawom
    sa adlaw, mas hayag sa bulan. Ikaw ang muduol na
    kapunawpunawan. Og sa presensya sa sagrado nga
    yuta, sa kamingawan sa bukid, sa kahilom sa sapa,
    mangayo kog pasaylo kanimo. Mag-ampo ko nga
    huktan nimo ang kini na mga pulong, ipalandong sa
    pagsubang sa adlaw.

9. Beloved, lead me by the crevices dramatized by the
    mirror. Let me find our skins undressed. Hold these
    fissures so I may confess. Might I venerate you with a
    litany of all the bits of my iniquities. Let me divulge all
    the ways I have lacerated a nerve. Consent to my
    recitation: the seven virtues before the seven deadly
    sins. Temperance before lust. Gratitude before
    gluttony. And what do I say about the acquiesence and
    chastity?

    *We elapse into touch without sensation. You stroke the
    curve of my torso leaving punctures without having to
    press. I feel your breath only through a memory of air. I
    spot a mark by your shoulders and I unfurl your arms.
    You look straight at the ceiling while I kiss you where it
    throbs.*

10. Ipinapaubaya ko na sa iyo ang pagsuko. Itinuturing ko
    nang pagmamay-ari itong kahangalan. Hindi natutupok
    ang pag-ibig, ito lamang ay nag-iiba ng kahulugan.
    Humiga tayo sa dalampasigan sa muling paglubog ng
    tubig alat, inilatag natin ang ating mga lumpong bahagi
    sa bandang hindi naaabot ng buwan. Sa gabing ito, tayo
    ay magiging anino. Linya linyang iginuhit ng nakaraan
    patungo sa magkahiwalay na patutungo. At doon tayo'y
    mag-iisip at matututo:

Sa gipalandongan,
          sa pag-ampo
sa himutok at mga kalyo
      ali sa di mahimutang na pagbana, sa kung aha ko
mubiya nimo
      alli na recuerdos del cobardia con este guerra

      Y entonces

          Ang pag-ibig,

               ay pag-ibig lamang.

Ang kawanangan ay isa na lamang walang kahulugang
paglutaw ng mga elemento. No hay ya cosa pa debe pidi na
universo.

      Hindi na gabay ang mga anino.
Hindi na tayo ang dating tayo.

      Ang mundo ay muli nang arbitraryo.

      Paquichura ta entra na entra'y medio?

tractions: experiments in Art Writing in June 2020
https://tractions-artwriting.medium.com/heteroglossia-
5052fa87125e

Wanda Phipps is a writer living in Brooklyn. Her books include *Mind Honey* (Autonomedia), *Field of Wanting: Poems of Desire* (BlazeVOX [books]), and *Wake-Up Calls: 66 Morning Poems* (Soft Skull Press). Her poetry has been published over a hundred times and translated into Ukrainian, Hungarian, Arabic, Galician and Bangla. She has received awards from the New York Foundation for the Arts, the National Theater Translation Fund, and others. As a founding member of Yara Arts Group she has collaborated on numerous theatrical productions presented in Ukraine, Kyrgyzstan, Siberia, and at La MaMa, E.T.C. in NYC. She's curated reading series at the Poetry Project at St. Mark's Church and written about the arts for *Boog City*, *Time Out New York*, *Paper Magazine*, and others.

no rose

the train is late again
so I'm late again
no surprise since it's
another wading through
mud day—a feet slowly sinking
in quicksand day
are my hands moving
more slowly too?
brain still flying?
body stiller than still
slower than slow?
where did this come from?
when did this fall down?
can I follow one thought
down its trail to now?
where everything matters
as little as anything else
what matters is to still
keep fighting the pull
towards paralysis
one fact—one thought
one perception at a time
until it passes or pauses
until the gears shift
back to normal
speed but now I feel
the pull—a heavy
anchor dragging—
a deep pain somewhere
close to the surface
all porcupined and
nettled—all thorns
and no rose

**Repsonse to Ukrainian poet Serhiy Zhadan's
"So I'm writing about her again"**

I am writing about him again
the mysterious one
and how we always
just miss each other

I can remember feeling a sensation
as someone passed me on the street
somehow, I knew him even though
we had never met, at least not in this life,
but still he had spoiled me for anyone else

my mind moved
carried by the wind
to thoughts like forbidden treats
memories still waiting to be made
moving the tides
washing over the shore

sweet, sweetheart, the wind
is wild tonight
and can't be tamed
sweet, sweetheart, my thoughts
are wild and have the strength
of ten thousand nights
of waves slowly wearing
away the edges of rocks,
cliffs, shifting sands

I remember your back
the broad sure back
of my mysterious one
which could bear all my burdens
support all my long-suffering days
and hold me up above the waves
sweet, sweetheart, you are
the dearest one, the most precious
memory I never had

sweet, sweetheart, you are my joy
my fleeting fire
my delicate smoke
under a bell jar

**Response to Ukrainian poet Serhiy Zhadan's
"In the summer she walks through the rooms"**

In the spring
he wanders through the halls
of his apartment
like a bad magician
each trick worse than the last.

He calls to the gods of magic
and they say,
"You are too practical—
your feet are too solidly
planted on the ground
to understand true magic
much less to really
be a magician."

But still he waves
his wand and hopes
for the best.

He proclaims
"Voila...Ta da...Presto!"
But nothing ever happens.
Scarves stay where they are.
Coins hide from the ears of children.
Cards remain comfortably
random in their cold decks
and all magic eludes him
like a shy lover.

**Response to Ukrainian poet Serhiy Zhadan's
"The best thing this winter"**

The worst thing this winter
was his footsteps in the first snow.
I watched them appear and disappear
as he left for the last time
and the snow fell and piled
high in those spaces that he left,
freezing into solid ice.

Sometimes I wish I had two hearts
one that remains calm and cool
and steady and one that
feels all the pain, all the loss,
all the grief of this life.

The worst thing this winter
was the sight of the trees
stripped bare of their leaves
like black-boned skeletons
against the ash grey skies.

The birds rarely found them
couldn't seem to settle
on their cold barren branches
and so I missed their morning songs
lost in the wind—lost in flight.

The worst thing that could have happened,
happened to us in that short time
between the first snow fall
and the moment those delicate flakes
lay crushed beneath your feet.

Serhiy Zhadan is an internationally known Ukrainian poet. He was born in the Luhansk Region of Ukraine and educated in Kharkiv, where he lives today. Responding to Russian's full-scale invasion of Ukraine, he organized local artists and musicians to deliver humanitarian aid in Kharkiv. He is the most popular poet in Ukraine and the author of seventeen books of poetry that have earned him numerous national and international awards. His poems and novels have been translated into over thirty languages. In 2022 Zhadan was awarded the Hannah Arendt Prize for Political Thought and the Peace Price from the German Book Trade. He has worked with Yara Arts Group since 2002 and is the front man for the band Zhadan and the Dogs.

English translations
by Virlana Tkacz and Wanda Phipps:

Virlana Tkacz heads the Yara Arts Group and has directed forty original shows at La MaMa Experimental Theatre in New York, as well as in Kyiv, Lviv, Kharkiv, Bishkek, Ulaanbaatar, and Ulan Ude. She was the curator on three major exhibits in Ukraine, including Kurbas: New Worlds at the Mystetskyi Arsenal in Kyiv. She received an NEA Poetry Translation Fellowship for her translations with Wanda Phipps of Serhiy Zhadan's poetry. She is the author of the book of poems *Three Wooden Trunks* (2022).

Wanda Phipps is a writer living in Brooklyn. Her books include *Mind Honey* (Autonomedia), *Field of Wanting: Poems of Desire* (BlazeVOX [books]), and *Wake-Up Calls: 66 Morning Poems* (Soft Skull Press). (See full bio on page 42.)

MAYBE IT'S TIME TO START

Maybe it's time to start.
I try to convince myself that it's not time,
that it's not right to blindly pronounce words
that haven't been spoken yet,
that haven't been printed,
no matter how much I choked
on the air this spring,
empty, wordless
no matter how much I choked
on the air this summer,
burning, without language
language is stronger than the fear of silence,
language should fill the breast pockets of life,
language should envelop places where people gather,
where they need to talk about themselves,
so that
they'll be recognized for their own voice.
Language sat in our lungs like a cold in March,
weighing us down like the clothes of fugitives
trying to cross a freezing river.
Deprived of a voice,
we weren't more honest with ourselves in silence.
We gave up our right to sing in the global choir,
afraid we'd sing a false note, afraid we'd miss the beat.
Silence stands behind us like an unsown field.
Speechless like wells filled with stones.
Maybe this -- our fear, our despair,
explains the desperate silence of embittered witnesses
who saw it all, who should testify,
sing out and name the killers,
call for justice.
Sound must be sown at midnight
to create the mist of morning song.
All this carries anxiety.
All this carries consequences.

June 15, 2022

FISH

Swim, dear fish, swim,
these are your islands,
this is your grass,
this is your guide
she sets your route,
she sews your parachute,
she guards the depths
near your rudder.

When the green stars
fall into the mouth of the river,
then your guide
will pronounce these words:
these are my dreams
these are fishing boats,
this is the night, this is the current
this is death – probably mine.

Life is silence and laughter.
Enough for everyone.
Enough for each of you.
Enough of my love for everyone.
So fly, dear fish, fly
I know all the bridges
I know all the lighthouses
and I do everything in reverse.

Only your words,
only secrets and marvels,
only fasting and confession
in a port city.
Love, dear fish, love,
even if it is hopeless,
even if there is no hope
rejoice, dear fish rejoice.

Love is worth it all --
worth all the pain
worth all the goodbyes

worth all the suffering and disgust
the howling of mad dogs,
the fury and mercy.
Worth more than life
and of course more than death.

2015

I IMAGINE HOW A BIRD SEES THIS

I imagine how a bird sees this:
dark river branch and winter roof tops
and the scattered pedestrians on the sidewalk.

I image how frightening it is for birds to fly over a river.

They always see the city from above.
Over the depot behind the station,
the yards,
the library on the other side of the river
on the written off pages of streets.

They repeat this February poem,
they know it from the gate to the attic,
they know where it will culminate,
and what will be the end – also.

Treading over the soil,
like treading over the lines on a face,
fish gather in the wetlands of the Donets River,
on the horizon
a dark tinge will flow down
there will be joy,
there will be reeds.

It's important to find warmth among people,
to love winter's handiwork,
the barely perceptible breath of the soil,
its seal.

You have to shout about this.
And so they shout.

2020